To My Child

With love from

Date

And now abide faith, hope, love, these three;
but the greatest of these is love.

I CORINTHIANS 13:13

Published in Nashville, Tennessee, by Tommy Nelson™, a division of Thomas Nelson, Inc.

Designed by Koechel Peterson & Associates, Minneapolis, Minnesota.

Scripture is taken from the *New King James Version.*
Copyright © 1982 by Thomas Nelson, Inc. Used by Permission. All rights reserved.

ISBN 0–8499–7571–9

Printed in the United States of America

00 01 02 03 04 RRD 9 8 7 6 5 4 3 2 1

Mother's Memories

TO HER CHILD

Featuring the art of THOMAS KINKADE

Written by Tama Fortner

Tommy
NELSON

Thomas Nelson, Inc.
Nashville

Dear Friend in God's Light,

If a man is fortunate, he develops an image of the ideal mother from the two most important women in his world: his own mother and the mother of his children.

My mother has been my number-one supporter since I was a schoolboy. She didn't just tape my earliest experiences with chalk and crayons on the refrigerator; she bought dime store frames and hung them in the living room next to our faded print of a Rembrandt masterwork. From the beginning, I was accustomed to thinking of my work as having value, as deserving of a place upon the wall. My mother continues to be delighted and moved by my artwork. When I unveiled my *Sunrise* painting, she was so overcome with emotion that she suddenly became weak and tearful and needed to be helped from the room.

When the inevitable crisis of confidence arose early in my career, and I wondered whether I had what it took to make it in this most uncertain of professions, the faith my mother had always displayed in my talents gave me the courage to persevere.

In all important respects, my mother is a woman of faith. As the head of a single-parent family, she often had to wrestle with financial challenges. But she was profoundly confident that God would provide. Often she would announce to the family some small "miracle"—perhaps a few extra dollars earned in her capacity as a notary public—which would get us through another week with groceries for the table. Thanks to her, I have always understood that miracles are an everyday evidence of God's goodness.

My wife Nanette further expanded my insights into the power and blessings of motherhood. Nanette is a wonderful mother to our children—understanding, loving, fully supportive. As I watch her nourish and nurture Merritt, Chandler, Winsor, and Everett, it occurs to me that a mother's challenge and triumph is not so very different from what confronts me as a painter.

Creating artwork is truly a faith endeavor. I enter my studio, approach my easel, and find myself face to face with a pristine white canvas. Through prayer and effort, I attempt to create a world of detail and color, of meaning and emotion on that blank canvas, using only the pigments on my palette, my brushes, and whatever skill and wisdom I've acquired.

In much the same way, a newborn enters the world as a blank slate, a clean canvas, with potential for joy and sorrow, for good or ill. The parents, and principally the mother, can color the canvas as God intends, using her boundless love and whatever skill and wisdom she's acquired. Like creating a painting, shaping the character of a child takes effort, perseverance, and most of all faith. Perhaps that's why, to me, a dedicated mother is nothing less than the greatest artist in the world.

God's blessings to all,

A MOTHER'S LOVE

Dearest Child,

The instant I first saw you, my life changed. Since then, my days have been filled with the coos of babyhood, the discoveries of toddlerhood, and the scraped-knee adventures of later childhood. There have been endless days of diapers and cookie crumbs, rounds of "But why, Mommy?"—and sometimes even flaring tempers—as you stretch your wings toward independence. But most of all, my heart has known more love than I ever knew was possible.

I thank my God
upon every remembrance of you.

PHILIPPIANS 1:3

Through this journal, I hope to give you an understanding of the person I used to be as well as the person I have become. I have tried to record my hopes and my dreams at this time in our lives, both for you and for myself. I want to share with you some of the secrets I have learned about life and love, faith and friendship, motherhood and childhood.

From our first moment together, I have thanked God for you. My prayer is that He will continue to watch over you long after the pages of this journal have yellowed and turned to dust. Know that I—and God—will love you forever.

Always,

_____

MY BIRTH

When and where I was born

My parents named me

What was happening in the world when I was born

The leader of the country was

I will praise You,
for I am fearfully and wonderfully made.

PSALM 139:14

My earliest memories

My mother's full maiden name

When and where she was born

My mother grew up in

My mother's best story about growing up

_____

_____

_____

_____

_____

_____

A favorite memory of my mother

_____

_____

_____

_____

_____

_____

I always think of my mother whenever

_____

_____

_____

_____

_____

_____

_____

_____

Her children rise up and call her blessed;
her husband also, and he praises her.

PROVERBS 31:28

FROM MY MOTHER

From my mother, I learned

My mother's greatest gift to me

My most memorable "woman-to-woman" talk with my mother

My mother taught me that God

She opens her mouth with wisdom,
And on her tongue is the law of kindness.

PROVERBS 31:26

My favorite recipe of my mother's

_____

_____

_____

_____

_____

_____

_____

_____

_____

_____

ABOUT MY FATHER *(Your Grandfather)*

My father's full name

_____

When and where he was born

_____

My father grew up in

_____

My father's best story about growing up

_____

_____

_____

_____

_____

_____

_____

_____

_____

_____

The righteous man walks in his integrity;
his children are blessed after him.

PROVERBS 20:7

My favorite memory of my father

I always think of my father whenever

15

FROM MY FATHER

From my father, I learned

The most wonderful thing about my father

He was especially good at

My father's greatest gift to me

My father taught me that God

Hear the instruction of your father.

PROVERBS 1:8

MY BROTHERS AND SISTERS

My brothers and sisters

The things we did together

Our greatest adventure growing up

Let brotherly love continue.

HEBREWS 13:1

I'll always remember

_____

_____

_____

As a child, my favorite family tradition was

_____

_____

_____

_____

_____

MY HOMETOWN

As a child, I lived in

_____

Our street was

_____

My favorite place in the neighborhood was

_____

_____

_____

_____

_____

My favorite community event

_____

_____

_____

_____

_____

_____

_____

_____

_____

_____

"You are the light of the world.
A city that is set on a hill cannot be hidden."
MATTHEW 5:14

Games my friends and I played

Someone from my hometown whom I admire

MY CHILDHOOD HOME

When I was growing up, our home was

My favorite place in our home

When I wanted to be alone

My favorite hiding place

My favorite place to play

At home I could always

I will dwell in the house of the LORD forever.

PSALM 23:6

Growing up, I usually spent my days

My chores included

On winter days, I would

On bright summer days, I liked to

For you were once darkness,
but now you are light in the Lord.
Walk as children of light.

EPHESIANS 5:8

During the day, my mother

_____

_____

_____

During the day, my father

_____

_____

_____

LIFE BACK THEN

An ice-cream cone cost

My favorite ice-cream flavor

Our family car(s)

The fashions of the day included

My favorite thing to wear

The child grew and became strong in spirit.

LUKE 1:80

The popular things to do

MY PETS

The first pet I ever owned

The pet I most loved

Other family pets

The pet I always wanted

Your righteousness is like the great mountains;
Your judgments are a great deep;
O LORD, You preserve man and beast.

PSALM 36:6

My favorite book or movie about an animal

My best animal story

CHILDHOOD TREASURES

My favorite storybook(s)

A game I never tired of playing

My favorite childhood rhyme

Every good gift and every perfect gift is from above,
and comes down from the Father of lights,
with whom there is no variation or shadow of turning.

JAMES 1:17

The best toy I ever owned

My most cherished item

31

SPIRITUAL BEGINNINGS

The first person who told me about God

As a child, my image of God was

I first knew that God was real when

My favorite religious holiday

People who helped me learn about God

*"You shall love the LORD your God
with all your heart, with all your soul,
and with all your mind."*

MATTHEW 22:37

My Favorite Scripture Verse As a Child

EARLY SCHOOL DAYS

The first school I attended

Other schools I attended

My favorite teacher during my early school years

My best subject(s)

A school experience I'll always remember

My best friend(s)

I wanted to grow up to be

Your word is a lamp to my feet
and a light to my path.

PSALM 119:105

HIGH SCHOOL YEARS

The school(s) I attended

My favorite teacher(s)

My friends

Popular fads

I dreamed of being

Get wisdom!
Get understanding!
PROVERBS 4:5

The most important thing(s) I learned

MUSIC

The musical instrument(s) I enjoyed most

As a young girl, I liked to listen to

During my teenage years, I preferred

Now, I enjoy

For your father and me, "our song"

Blessed are the people who know the joyful sound!

PSALM 89:15

FIRST TIMES

The first time I wore makeup

The first time I drove a car

My first job

My first time to live away from home

We love Him because He first loved us.

1 JOHN 4:19

My first dream of being a mom

_____

_____

_____

_____

_____

_____

_____

_____

_____

FRIENDSHIP

God tells us that true friendship is

The friend that I've had the longest

A friend who feels like a sister

The friend I wish I hadn't lost touch with

The friend who makes me laugh the most

The greatest gift a friend has ever given me

You are one of my best friends because

There is a friend who sticks closer than a brother.

PROVERBS 18:24

ROMANCE

My first crush

My first boyfriend

My first real date

My first kiss

My first broken heart

Oh, give thanks to the LORD,
for He is good!

PSALM 107:1

The funniest thing that ever happened on a date

TRAVELS

The farthest I have ever been from home

_____

_____

_____

_____

The best vacation from my childhood

_____

_____

_____

_____

My favorite place I've been

I have always dreamed of going

The best vacation I've had with you

The place I would most like us to see together

"The LORD your God
is with you wherever you go."
JOSHUA 1:9

MY FAITH

For me, God has always

I have learned that faith is

I sense the presence of God when

For by grace you have been saved through faith,
and that not of yourselves;
it is the gift of God.

EPHESIANS 2:8

I hope I have taught you that God is

One thing I want you to always remember is

My Favorite Scripture Verse about God

_____
_____
_____
_____
_____

LESSONS IN LOVE

As a child, I believed that love

Over the years, I have learned

My mother taught me that love

My father showed me that love

The most difficult lesson for me to learn about love

Let all that you do be done with love.

1 CORINTHIANS 16:14

FALLING IN LOVE

My first impression of your father

Our first date

I fell in love with him because

My favorite thing about your father

Beloved, let us love one another, for love is of God.

1 JOHN 4:7

He proposed by

For your own marriage, I pray that

OUR WEDDING DAY

The day, time, and place we were married

What I wore

My attendants

What they wore

My most vivid memory of our wedding

For our honeymoon we went to

"For wherever you go, I will go;
And wherever you lodge, I will lodge;
Your people shall be my people,
And your God, my God."

RUTH 1:16

NEWLYWEDS

Our first home

Our first real disagreement was over

One thing we still laugh about

The most difficult thing to adjust to

Love . . . bears all things, believes all things,
hopes all things, endures all things.

I CORINTHIANS 13:4,7

The best thing about being married

THEN CAME YOU

When I first learned you were coming into our lives

Your father's reaction

Your name is special because

When I first saw you, I prayed

A PHOTO

OF YOU

Behold, children are a heritage from the LORD.

PSALM 127:3

THE JOYS OF MOTHERHOOD

The thing I love most about being your mother

The most surprising thing about being a mother

The first time I saw you

"Whoever receives one little child . . .
in My name receives Me."
MATTHEW 18:5

One of my favorite memories of you

When you become a parent, I hope that you will remember

WATCHING YOU GROW UP

As a child, you

As you grew older, you

I was so proud of you when

You tested your independence by

The person you are now is someone

I pray that

I have no greater joy than to hear that
my children walk in truth.

PLAY TIME

Always remember to take time to play because

_____
_____
_____
_____
_____

When you were little, our favorite game to play together

_____
_____
_____
_____
_____

The hobby I enjoy most

_____
_____
_____
_____
_____

You have put gladness in my heart.

PSALM 4:7

I would like to teach you

I hope that you will teach me

CELEBRATING CHRISTMAS

Our first Christmas with you

_____

_____

_____

_____

My favorite Christmas tradition for our family

_____

_____

_____

_____

_____

_____

_____

My favorite thing about Christmas

_____

_____

_____

_____

_____

Thanks be to God for His indescribable gift!

2 CORINTHIANS 9:15

My best Christmas recipe

MY DREAMS FOR YOU

When you were born, I dreamed of you becoming

Now, my greatest dream for you is

Dreams are important because

"All things are possible to him who believes."

MARK 9:23

One dream you have made come true

One of the things I admire about you is

MY PROMISES TO YOU

As your mother, I promise

_____

_____

_____

_____

_____

I hope that you will promise

_____

_____

_____

_____

Although we disagree sometimes, I will always

_____

_____

_____

_____

_____

Trust in the LORD *with all your heart, . . .*
And He shall direct your paths.

PROVERBS 3:5–6

I hope that together we will

_____
_____
_____
_____
_____

You can always trust God to

_____
_____
_____
_____
_____

My Favorite Promise from God

_____

_____

_____

_____

_____

MY FAVORITE THINGS

My favorite time of day

My favorite season

My favorite book

My favorite movie

My favorite story from the Bible

"For where your treasure is, there your heart will be also."

MATTHEW 6:21

That which I cherish most in this life

_____

_____

_____

_____

_____

Something that I didn't like as a child, but is now a favorite

_____

_____

_____

_____

QUIET TIMES WITH GOD

Through prayer, I have found

For me, the best time of day to pray is

My favorite place to pray

_____
_____
_____
_____

I know that God hears my prayers because

_____
_____
_____
_____
_____
_____
_____

My ever-present prayer for you is

_____
_____
_____
_____
_____
_____
_____
_____

Pray without ceasing.

1 THESSALONIANS 5:17

My Favorite Prayer

_____

_____

_____

_____

_____

_____

_____

_____

Being a parent

When you have a child, be sure to

Always be ready to

Show your love by

Behold what manner of love the Father has bestowed on us,
that we should be called children of God!

I JOHN 3:1

Teach your child to

WINNING AT LIFE

I believe that God gave us life so that we could

_____

_____

_____

_____

_____

To be a success in life

_____

_____

_____

_____

_____

I believe you are a success because

_____

_____

_____

_____

_____

_____

"But seek first the kingdom of God and His righteousness,
and all these things shall be added to you."

MATTHEW 6:33

When life is hectic and hurried, remember

AS I GROW OLDER

The things that I once believed were important

With each passing year, I appreciate more

One thing I wish I had done differently growing up

One thing I wish I had done differently as an adult

When I was young, I worried that

But now I realize that

I applied my heart to know,
To search and seek out wisdom
and the reason of things.
ECCLESIASTES 7:25

MY THOUGHTS ABOUT HEAVEN

I believe that heaven is

The thing(s) that I most look forward to about heaven

When I get to heaven, the question(s) that I most want to ask God

"Rejoice because your names are written in heaven."

LUKE 10:20

I believe that in order to get to heaven, a person must

FAMILY TIES

You and I are most alike in that

We are most different in that

The person you remind me of most

Family is important because

With your own family, I hope you

And be kind to one another,
tenderhearted, forgiving one another.

EPHESIANS 4:32

Our Family Tree

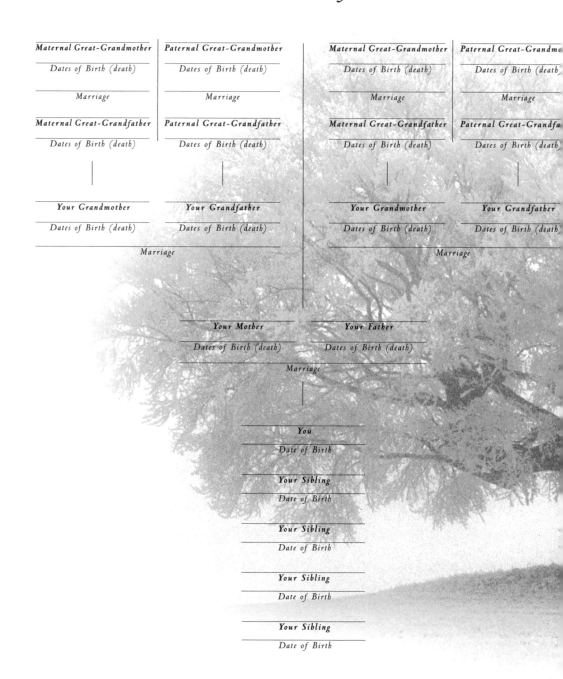

Maternal Great-Grandmother
Dates of Birth (death)
Marriage
Maternal Great-Grandfather
Dates of Birth (death)

Paternal Great-Grandmother
Dates of Birth (death)
Marriage
Paternal Great-Grandfather
Dates of Birth (death)

Maternal Great-Grandmother
Dates of Birth (death)
Marriage
Maternal Great-Grandfather
Dates of Birth (death)

Paternal Great-Grandmother
Dates of Birth (death)
Marriage
Paternal Great-Grandfather
Dates of Birth (death)

Your Grandmother
Dates of Birth (death)

Your Grandfather
Dates of Birth (death)

Your Grandmother
Dates of Birth (death)

Your Grandfather
Dates of Birth (death)

Marriage

Marriage

Your Mother
Dates of Birth (death)

Your Father
Dates of Birth (death)

Marriage

You
Date of Birth

Your Sibling
Date of Birth

Your Sibling
Date of Birth

Your Sibling
Date of Birth

Your Sibling
Date of Birth

A Favorite Photo of Our Family

PLACE
PHOTO
HERE

Now may the Lord of peace Himself give you
peace always in every way.

2 THESSALONIANS 3:16

INDEX OF PAINTINGS